EXPLORING CIVIL

THE BEGINNINGS
1948

SELENE CASTROVILLA

Franklin Watts®
An imprint of Scholastic Inc.

Content Consultant

A special thank you to Ryan M. Jones at the National Civil Rights Museum
for his expert consultation.

Library of Congress Cataloging-in-Publication Data
Names: Castrovilla, Selene, 1966- author.
Title: The beginnings : 1948 / by Selene Castrovilla.
Other titles: Exploring civil rights.
Description: First edition. | New York : Franklin Watts, an imprint of
  Scholastic Inc., 2022. | Series: Exploring civil rights | Includes
  bibliographical references and index. | Audience: Ages 10–14 | Audience:
  Grades 7–9 | Summary: "Series continuation. Narrative nonfiction, key
  events of the Civil Rights Movement in the years spanning from
  1939–1954. Photographs throughout"— Provided by publisher.
Identifiers: LCCN 2022002628 (print) | LCCN 2022002629 (ebook) |
  ISBN 9781338800593 (library binding) | ISBN 9781338800609 (paperback) |
  ISBN 9781338800616 (ebk)
Subjects: LCSH: African Americans—Civil rights—History—Juvenile
  literature. | Civil rights movements—United States—History—20th
  century—Juvenile literature. | Civil rights workers—United
  States—Juvenile literature. | BISAC: JUVENILE NONFICTION / History /
  United States / 20th Century | JUVENILE NONFICTION / History / United
  States / General
Classification: LCC E185.61 .C2928 2022 (print) | LCC E185.61 (ebook) |
  DDC 323.1196/073—dc23/eng/20220131
LC record available at https://lccn.loc.gov/2022002628
LC ebook record available at https://lccn.loc.gov/2022002629

10 9 8 7 6 5 4 3 2 1   23 24 25 26 27

Printed in China   62
First edition, 2023

Composition by Kay Petronio

COVER & TITLE PAGE: June 30,
1948, President Harry S. Truman
signs a resolution making
February 1 an annual holiday:
"National Freedom Day."

President Truman campaigns for reelection, page 66.

Table of Contents

Mahalia Jackson, p. 56.

African Americans did not receive fair trials under Jim Crow laws, and many were unjustly imprisoned.

The Way It Was

In the period directly following the American Civil War (1861–1865), three **amendments** to the U.S. Constitution sought to grant African Americans the rights they'd been denied during slavery. In 1865, the Thirteenth Amendment abolished slavery. In 1868, the Fourteenth Amendment granted **citizenship** to African Americans. And in 1870, the Fifteenth Amendment gave African American men the right to vote.

Despite those triumphs, this period also saw the introduction of Black codes, or laws passed to limit the rights and freedoms of Black Americans. They soon became known as **Jim Crow** laws, and they were especially strict in the American South. Jim Crow laws controlled where people of color could live and work.

Jim Crow laws enforced **segregation**. Under the racial policy of "separate but equal," Black Americans could be given separate facilities if the quality was equal to the white facilities. In reality, however, there was no equality. African Americans were forced to attend separate and inadequate schools, live in run-down neighborhoods, and even drink from rusty or broken public water fountains.

In 1896, a group of **activists** tried to overturn the Jim Crow laws with the Supreme Court case *Plessy v. Ferguson*. Unfortunately, when the case was lost, Jim Crow laws became even more acceptable across the country, but remained most prominent in the southern United States.

The Fight Begins

As Jim Crow expanded, two prominent **civil rights** organizations emerged. The National Association of Colored Women's Clubs (NACWC) was founded in 1896 by a group of politically active women, including Harriet Tubman. Members of the association dedicated themselves to fighting for voting rights and for ending racial violence in the form of **lynchings** against African Americans. In addition to lynchings, African Americans suffered severe harassment, beatings, and even bombings at the hands of racist organizations like the **Ku Klux Klan** (KKK), who had millions of members in the 1920s.

The National Association for the Advancement of Colored People (NAACP), founded in 1909, followed in the NACWC's footsteps. The NAACP focused on opposing segregation and Jim Crow policies. Both organizations would be crucial in the coming fight for justice.

1948

The civil rights movement was just taking shape in 1948, and President Harry S. Truman helped set its course. Truman's support for Black Americans was unusual in the **federal** government and was something many leaders did not want. Despite the backlash it caused, Truman insisted it was the government's duty to protect America's Black citizens from the hate and **discrimination** they faced and ensure their freedoms. The Supreme Court would make a landmark decision against housing discrimination in the *Shelley v. Kraemer* case. Activist A. Philip Randolph pushed Truman to sign an executive order to end military segregation. And Alice Coachman would make history to become the first Black woman to win a gold medal at the 1948 Summer Olympics. ∎

President Truman speaks up for civil rights during his 1948 State of the Union address, putting him at odds with much of Congress.

1

Time to Act

President Harry S. Truman entered 1948 with civil rights on his mind. His heart was heavy with the violence and discrimination African Americans continually faced, especially in the southern states. It was time for the federal government to protect its Black citizens and provide them with the equal rights they deserved. Truman planned on making a strong statement in his January 7th State of the Union Address. The State of the Union Address is a speech the U.S. president must deliver to Congress at the start of each year to let members know what is happening in the country and recommend new laws and policies for solving the nation's problems. Truman knew publicly supporting civil rights would hurt him politically—and this was an election year. In his mind, though, equality was more important than politics, and he would not— *he could not*—let the gross injustices continue.

A Long Way from Missouri

Harry S. Truman was born in Missouri in 1884—
nearly 20 years after enslavement had been abolished. His grandparents on both sides supported
slavery and had enslaved African Americans.

Truman's family moved several times while he
was young, finally settling in Independence, a segregated Missouri town. Raised in a racist environment,
Truman grew up to have racist views, too.

But Truman also knew what it was like to be
the underdog. His family was poor, and he couldn't
afford college. He understood the difficulty of over-
coming poverty.

When Truman became president in 1945,
southern members of
Congress were sure
that he would support
continued segregation.
In the summer of 1946,
Truman received a letter
from civil rights leader
and former military

10-year-old
Harry Truman.

officer Richard R. Wright. This letter changed Truman's long-held opinions, and it would shape the course of his presidency.

Truman Reacts

Wright's letter described the brutal attack on Black World War II veteran Isaac Woodard on February 12, 1946. Woodard was traveling home by bus after being honorably discharged by the United States Army. Still in uniform, Woodard was assaulted by South Carolina police, including Police Chief Lynwood Shull. They clubbed his eyes, permanently blinding him. No one had been arrested in the case.

Shaken and outraged by this attack on a man who had just put his life on the line for America, Truman agreed to meet with the National Emergency Committee Against Mob Violence, a group formed of civil rights activists, **labor** activists, and religious leaders, on September 19, 1946. NAACP executive secretary Walter White, leader of the group, read Truman a list of lynchings that had happened across

Boxing champion Joe Louis (left) helped organize a fundraising event for WWII veteran Isaac Woodard (center).

the country. Truman initiated a federal investigation into the Woodard hate crime. Shull was arrested and tried in the South Carolina federal court. An all-white jury declared Shull not guilty.

Freedom from Fear

Rocked by Shull's acquittal, Truman established the President's Committee on Civil Rights (PCCR) by Executive Order 9808 on December 5, 1946. He called this order "Freedom from Fear." The 15-member **interracial** PCCR was tasked with analyzing the state of civil rights in America, investigating mob violence, and proposing legislation to protect civil rights. Truman told the committee members, "We're making progress, but we're not making progress fast enough." He gave them a deadline of one year.

Landmark Ruling

The Supreme Court delivered a **unanimous** ruling on January 12, 1948. Their verdict in *Sipuel v. Board of Regents of the University of Oklahoma* declared that the state of Oklahoma must provide instruction for Black and white students, requiring the admission of qualified Black students to previously all-white state law schools. This reversed a decision by the Supreme Court of Oklahoma that barred Black students from being admitted.

Ada Sipuel Fisher knew she was delaying her legal career when she applied to the all-white University of Oklahoma on January 14, 1946. She was willing to do this in order to challenge segregation. As she expected, she was denied admission because of her race. She began her legal challenge, which took two years to reach the Supreme Court. Arguments were made in front of the Court on January 7–8, 1948. With remarkable speed, the Court returned with their decision in four days. The NAACP Legal Defense Fund's Thurgood Marshall was one of Fisher's attorneys in this landmark early civil rights case.

Ada Sipuel Fisher (right) speaks with her lawyers, Amos Hall (left) and Thurgood Marshall.

Walter White invited Truman to speak at the NAACP's annual meeting in Washington, DC. Truman accepted.

More than 10,000 NAACP members lined the Lincoln Memorial Reflecting Pool on the National Mall on June 29, 1947. Truman addressed them from the steps of the Lincoln Memorial, and his speech was broadcast by radio. He said that civil rights were a moral priority and his priority for the federal government. He closed by quoting Lincoln's promise that the country would be a source of benefits for all.

Truman was the first American president to address the NAACP at the meeting—and the first president to declare the equality of Black Americans. White compared Truman's speech to Lincoln's Gettysburg Address.

"We must and shall guarantee the civil rights of all our citizens," Truman told members of the NAACP at the Lincoln Memorial.

To Secure These Rights

On October 29, 1947, the PCCR delivered a 178-page document entitled "To Secure These Rights: The Report of the President's Committee on Civil Rights." The title of the report came from a line in the Declaration of Independence, the statement signed by the Second Continental Congress on July 4, 1776, announcing America's separation from England. The message was clear: Governments were supposed to protect their citizens' rights.

The committee had gathered information through public hearings and private meetings. They conducted studies and received communications from hundreds of citizens.

The report analyzed specific rights, and how African Americans were being denied them. It also described lynchings and other hate crimes against Black citizens. The committee believed that more Americans must be made aware "of the gulf between our civil rights principles and our practices."

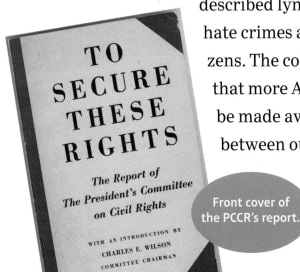

Front cover of the PCCR's report.

E. Franklin Frazier

Professor E. Franklin Frazier took office as the first Black president of the American Sociological Society on January 1, 1948. Frazier had been a founding member of the District of Columbia Sociological Society, serving as its president in 1943 and 1944. The following year, he served as president of the Eastern Sociological Society.

"Sociology is the study of social life, social change, and the social causes and consequences of human behavior," explains the society. Frazier, a teacher of English, history, mathematics, and French, was earning his master's degree at Clark University when he learned about sociology. He wrote a thesis titled "New Currents of Thought Among the Colored People of America." Plunging into sociology, he switched the course of his career, studying in the U.S. and overseas, and earning his PhD.

E. Franklin Frazier's book *The Negro Family in the United States* (1939) was one of the first works addressing African Americans by a Black author.

It called for the establishment of a permanent civil rights **commission**, the Joint Congressional Committee on Civil Rights, and the Civil Rights Division in the Department of Justice. More solutions included federal protection from lynching, a permanent fair employment practices commission, and the end of poll taxes (where voters were required to pay a tax when they voted).

Truman's shocking **endorsement** of civil rights severed his relationship with fellow Southern Democrats.

Truman was determined to follow the blueprint the committee offered for the federal government to enact legislation. He resolved that 1948 would be a year of action toward justice for African Americans.

State of the Union

On January 7, 1948, President Truman addressed Congress with his State of the Union speech as the PCCR's report dominated his mind. The address was broadcast to every home in America—and Truman made his intentions for civil rights reform clear.

Proposing that the federal government work toward goals that would have the greatest significance for "the foundations of our **democracy** and the happiness of our people." Truman said that to deny human rights was to deny the basic beliefs of democracy.

Truman stated that some American citizens were still being denied equal opportunities for education, jobs and economic advancement, and voting. Most seriously, some citizens were being denied equal protection under the law.

Closing his statement on civil rights by mentioning the PCCR recent report, Truman stated that it "points the way to corrective action by the Federal Government and by State and local governments." He said he would send a special message to Congress about this important subject.

Truman said, "Discrimination is a disease, we must attack it wherever it appears."

Truman knew that most members of Congress did not share his conviction that civil rights must be addressed. The 1946 United States elections had given control of Congress to the Republicans. Although their party had backed civil rights previously, they were determined to block legislation that might help Truman—a Democrat—win reelection in November. The Southern Democrats cared more about keeping segregation intact than supporting their party's president. Nevertheless, Truman hoped that once he sent that message to Congress, revealing how bad the present situation was for Black Americans and how the government could help, the members would be swayed to act. He would soon learn, however, that some people's **prejudices** could *not* be reversed. ▪

South Carolina's Governor J. Strom Thurmond was the Southern Democrats' candidate for president in the 1948 race.

2

Reform Meets Resistance

President Truman's State of the Union address
alerted Southern Democrats to trouble ahead.
They had no intention of letting the president get
any civil rights legislation passed. Jim Crow laws
suited them well, and **desegregation** was a threat
to their way of life.

On January 20, 1948, Fielding L. Wright took
office as governor of Mississippi. He used his inau-
gural address to voice the first public southern
outcry against Truman's intentions for civil rights.
He said that Truman's proposed policies would
"wreck the South and its institutions," which he
pledged to protect. Wright called on Southern
Democrats to abandon their party.

We Need Only the Will

President Truman sent his special message on civil rights to Congress on February 2. He asked members to support and enact the necessary civil rights laws. The laws should be based on the findings and recommendations of the PCCR. He wrote, "There is a serious gap between our ideals and some of our practices. This gap must be closed."

Among the specific requests he made were to better protect the right to vote, to establish a Fair Employment Practices Commission to prevent unfair discrimination, and to end discrimination in interstate transportation facilities.

Truman wrote passionately about protecting lives. "A specific Federal measure is needed to deal with the crime of lynching—against which I cannot speak too strongly . . . . So long as one person walks in fear of lynching, we shall not have achieved equal justice under law. I call upon the Congress to take decisive action against this crime."

Mississippi governor Fielding L. Wright.

Lynchings were public events, like this one in 1936 of Rainey Bethea, a 26-year-old African American man in Owensboro, Kentucky.

Truman closed his emotional message with the words, "We know the way. We need only the will."

Strong Reactions

Southern governors gathered in Wakulla Springs, Florida, on February 7 to discuss strategy against civil rights. Once again, Governor Wright proposed that they immediately leave the Democratic Party and start their own political party. James Folsom, Alabama's governor, wanted more time before acting. He suggested that they wait until July's Democratic convention to challenge Truman and his civil rights proposals. The governor of South Carolina, J. Strom Thurmond, delivered a motion to send a group to

Governor of Alabama James E. Folsom.

Democratic National Committee Chairman J. Howard McGrath.

speak with Democratic national chairman J. Howard McGrath about their concerns. This seemed like a good compromise to the group, who voted in favor of Thurmond's proposal. He would head the group of five later that month.

On February 8, Reverend James Hinton, South Carolina's NAACP president, wrote to Thurmond protesting the governor's role in opposing civil rights. He said that South Carolina's African American citizens wanted the end of lynchings and a chance for equal job opportunities. He asked Thurmond to "denounce and condemn the stand of the Southern Governors."

Voter Suppression

At least 300 white men and women who belonged to the Ku Klux Klan held a parade in the center of Wrightsville, Georgia, on March 2, 1948. They burned crosses on the county courthouse lawn and spewed racial hate and violence in speeches. A local **primary** election was approaching to choose the county sheriff and the city court judge. The KKK event was held with the intention of terrifying and deterring the county's 400 Black registered voters from casting their ballots. Their tactics worked: No Black citizens voted in the primary and the Black community was accused of a lack of interest in county affairs.

Hooded members of the KKK burn a cross on the courthouse lawn in Wrightsville, GA, on March 2, 1948, to frighten Black citizens from voting.

Rev. James Hinton (far right), president of South Carolina's NAACP, with other South Carolina NAACP leaders.

Thurmond had never been publicly opposed to civil rights. But the opportunity for political gain was too much for Thurmond to pass up. He turned his back on the NAACP and instead saw a chance for greatness—he even imagined a run for the U.S. presidency.

Speaking from the Senate floor on February 9, Senator James Eastland of Mississippi rejected President Truman's civil rights proposal. He declared that the people of the South should not sit by while the "white race is destroyed."

On February 11, 100 Black Mississippi leaders met in a Jackson church for a statewide mass meeting. They passed two **resolutions**. First, they sent a telegram to Truman, supporting his civil rights program.

Second, they **petitioned** Governor Wright and the state legislature to establish a permanent interracial commission to work out a plan for greater equality among all citizens. Wright and the members of the legislature ignored this petition, not even acknowledging its receipt. Nevertheless, this meeting was a milestone for the

Senator James Eastland of Mississippi.

Black community in Mississippi. It was the first time African Americans went on record in the state asking for their civil rights.

Resist Them We Will

Although the southern governors agreed to wait before acting, Governor Wright had already organized a statewide meeting of Mississippi Democrats before he headed to Florida. On February 12, at least 4,000 people gathered in Jackson, Mississippi, where they booed Truman's name. They voted unanimously for a resolution rejecting Truman's civil rights proposals. Judge Herbert Holmes chaired the Mississippi State Democratic Executive Committee.

Southern Hate

Senator James Eastland of Mississippi, a fierce opponent of Truman's civil rights proposals, as well as a wealthy **plantation** owner and **white supremacist**, successfully led a campaign to block an anti-lynching bill on January 21, 1948. This bill would have made lynchings a federal crime, holding lynch mob members and local law enforcement officers legally accountable for participating in these murders.

Eastland refused to acknowledge that law enforcement had participated in the lynchings of thousands of African Americans.

During the meeting on January 21, Eastland said there was no need for the bill because "we don't have any lynchings now." In reality, more than four dozen lynchings had been recorded in the 1940s—six of them in Eastland's home state.

Eastland's father had participated in a double lynching in 1904, the year Eastland was born. The lynch mob captured and lynched a Black man named Luther Holbert and his wife, Mary Holbert. No one was ever arrested for their deaths. Holbert had been suspected of killing Eastland's uncle, a plantation owner. He never received a trial determining whether he was in fact guilty of that crime.

Senator Eastland opposed civil rights legislation in the Senate for three decades.

A Black family in Mississippi.

Holmes stated that he would begin organizing a nationwide meeting in opposition to Truman and his ideals.

On February 20, about 50 legislatures from 11 southern states met secretly on Capitol Hill to declare war on Truman's civil rights agenda. They resolved to cooperate with the southern governors in whatever actions they decided to take. The states represented were Alabama, Arkansas, Florida, Georgia, Louisiana, Mississippi, North Carolina, South Carolina, Tennessee, Texas, and Virginia.

Thurmond and his four fellow southern governors' **delegates** met with McGrath on February 23.

J. Howard McGrath (right) and the Democratic Party remained loyal to President Truman and committed to his reelection.

The meeting did not go the way they wanted. While remaining polite, McGrath made it clear that the Democratic Party supported Truman and his policies.

The following day, the outraged southern governors announced the Southern Democrats' united opposition to the "so-called civil-rights program" Truman had proposed.

On March 13, the southern governors met in Washington, DC. They unanimously passed a resolution denouncing the Democratic Party leadership for its support of civil rights. They advised citizens of southern states to fight to prevent the presidential nomination or vice presidential nomination of any person who supported federal civil rights legislation, taking away each state's choices in the matter.

In Good Cause

Some Southern Democrats met privately with Truman, telling him that everything would work out for him if he would soften his views. In other words, they would back his reelection if he stopped his insistence on civil rights. Truman declined. He received a letter from an old friend in Missouri suggesting that he back away from civil rights. Truman wrote back, "I am asking for equality of opportunity for all human beings, and as long as I stay here, I am going to continue that fight." ∎

African Americans supporting Truman's reelection.

Civil rights activist A. Philip Randolph campaigns for Black men to refuse serving in the U.S. Army until it is desegregated.

3

Pressure on All Sides

On March 22, civil rights activist A. Philip Randolph and other members of the Committee Against Jim Crow in Military Service and Training met with President Truman at the White House, at Truman's invitation. Randolph told Truman that he had traveled around the United States, and expressed that African American soldiers would be more willing to fight for their country overseas if they were treated fairly at home.

Truman was disturbed by that statement. But more than that, he was strongly moved by it. He asked Randolph what needed to be done.

Randolph replied, "Well, some action ought to be taken in the form of an **executive order** barring and banning Jim Crow in the Armed Forces, eliminating discrimination and segregation." Truman said, "I agree with you."

A Call to Disobey

Randolph had teamed with New York State official Grant Reynolds to form the committee after a peacetime **draft** and universal military training were proposed in 1947. Universal military training was a program designed to provide training for all American males after they turned 18. The committee planned on urging Black men to disobey the draft if the armed forces weren't desegregated. They also planned to hold protests demanding equal treatment for Black soldiers in the United States armed forces.

Randolph wrote a follow-up letter to Truman, reminding him about the Committee on Civil Rights'

Randolph (right) leads this protest outside the Democratic National Convention in Philadelphia, PA, on July 12, 1948.

THE RIGHT TO WOR

At a New York City rally inside Madison Square Garden, Randolph demands fair employment practices for Black citizens.

recommendations to provide equality to all American citizens. This included members of the military. He ended his letter asking for an executive order ceasing all discrimination in the armed forces.

On March 31, Randolph testified before the Senate Committee on Armed Services on the issue of universal military training. He told the committee if there was a draft without desegregating the armed forces, Black men would refuse to sign up for it.

The NAACP did not endorse Randolph's position. They were worried that this rigid stance would harm the chances for Truman's civil rights proposals to pass. But African American youth were on board. Seventy-one percent of 2,200 Black college students polled by the NAACP agreed with Randolph's position. Would they serve if there was a war or emergency? Eighty-two percent of the students said yes, but

Randolph (right) and Grant Reynolds testify against army segregation at the Senate Armed Services Committee in 1948.

fifty-one percent said that they would only serve if the discrimination and segregation ended.

Major Victories for Civil Rights

On May 3, the Supreme Court handed down a landmark decision against housing discrimination. Delivering its ruling for *Shelley v. Kraemer*, the Court declared that racially discriminating property restrictions could not be upheld by the state courts.

Property restrictions were used by landowners to limit how their property could be used and sold. Some of these restrictions were created specifically to prevent people of certain races from buying or renting the property. While such restrictions were not illegal for citizens to create, the Supreme Court ruled that it was **unconstitutional** for states or the federal government to enforce them.

Play Ball!

On April 20, 1948, Roy Campanella became the first African American catcher in Major League Baseball (MLB), playing with the Brooklyn Dodgers against the New York Giants. He was only the second Black player in the major leagues after Jackie Robinson.

Campanella moved from the Negro National League (NNL) into the Brooklyn Dodgers' minor league system in 1946. Campanella was a hard worker and had an easygoing personality. He was considered for becoming the first Black MLB player—but Robinson was ultimately chosen.

Campanella began playing for the Washington Elite Giants in the NNL in 1937, at age 15. He dropped out of school at age 16 so he could play full time. He was a star player with Washington until 1945.

From 1949 to 1956, he was picked for the MLB All-Star Game every year. In 1949, he was one of the first four African Americans chosen. In 1950, he hit home runs in five straight games—a feat unmatched until 2001. Campanella received the Most Valuable Player (MVP) award in the National League in 1951, 1953, and 1955. He helped the Dodgers win their first World Series championship in 1955.

Brooklyn Dodgers' catcher Roy Campanella led the way for African American baseball players to join Major League Baseball.

The Shelley family fought to keep their home and won.

The Fourteenth Amendment guarantees "equal protection under the law."

Shelley v. Kraemer was actually four cases combined and argued together before the Court. They had been combined because they were all property restrictions cases. The other cases were *McGhee v. Sipes, Hurd v. Hodge*, and *Urciolo v. Hodge*.

The Shelleys, a Black family, bought a St. Louis, Missouri, home in 1945. They did not know the property had a restriction in place forbidding Black citizens from living there. Louis Kraemer, a white property owner who lived 10 blocks away, sued to stop the Shelleys from moving in based on the restriction. The Supreme Court of Missouri ruled that the restriction was enforceable by law. George L. Vaughn, an African American lawyer devoted to improving lives in the Black community, represented the Shelleys. He appealed the case to the U.S. Supreme Court.

The following week, on May 10, the Supreme Court would also rule that property belonging to a church could not be restricted to "white only" use. In 1945, the Monroe Avenue Church of Christ in Columbus, Ohio, had purchased a house for their pastor, who was "partially" African American. That property had a restriction stating that only white people could live there. Citing their previous ruling in *Shelley v. Kraemer*, the justices said that any racial property restrictions were unconstitutional.

The Fight Is On

On May 9, Governor Wright addressed the Black population of Mississippi on the radio. He told them that no matter what President Truman recommended and regardless of any laws Congress would ever pass, African Americans would never achieve civil rights in their state. He essentially advised Mississippi's Black residents to move to another state.

Hit Song

Jazz singer Nat King Cole's recording of the song "Nature Boy" was released on March 29, 1948, as a single by Capitol Records, and later appeared on the album *The Nat King Cole Story*. The song helped Cole reach a wider audience by propelling him onto the pop music charts, which was difficult for a Black artist at that time.

"Nature Boy" debuted on the Billboard pop charts on April 16, 1948, remaining there for 15 weeks. It peaked at number one. It also reached number two on the Rhythm & Blues, or R&B, charts. "Nature Boy" sold a million copies in 1948. Billboard DJs named it the greatest record of the year and it put Cole into the musical spotlight for all Americans.

Nat King Cole would accumulate over 100 hits on the pop charts.

Mississippi "Dixiecrats" walk out of the Democratic National Convention on July 14, 1948.

The next day, Wright hosted 3,500 Southern Democrats, or "Dixiecrats," in a meeting they called the States' Rights Convention. The main street in Jackson was lined with **Confederate** flags to welcome these guests.

Keynote speaker Governor Thurmond declared that the South was in a revolt against the present leadership of the Democratic Party. He stated, "The fight is on." They would not rest until that leadership was gone and claimed that the South could not be forced to desegregate.

The conference attendees set out to rewrite the Democratic Party's future without mentioning civil rights. They would present it to the National Democratic Convention on July 12. If the Democratic

Party refused to accept their version—and if the party nominated Harry S. Truman as its presidential candidate—they would hold their own convention on July 17 in Birmingham, Alabama.

Undercover in the South

Also in May, award-winning white reporter Ray Sprigle of the *Pittsburgh Post-Gazette* posed as an African American man to learn what life was like for people living under the South's Jim Crow laws.

With the help of the NAACP's Walter White, Sprigle spent a month traveling through the Deep South. When he returned, he published a 21-part series: "I Was a Negro in the South for 30 Days."

Preparing for the journey, Sprigle tried many methods to darken his skin, including walnut juice and chemicals. Nothing worked. Finally, he went to Florida, shaved his head and mustache,

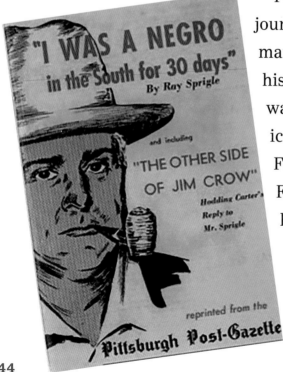

"I WAS A NEGRO in the South for 30 days"
By Ray Sprigle

and including

"THE OTHER SIDE OF JIM CROW"
Hodding Carter's Reply to Mr. Sprigle

reprinted from the

Pittsburgh Post-Gazette

Ray Sprigle adapted his experiences posing as a Black man in the South into a book.

and spent three weeks developing a dark tan so he could pass for a light-skinned Black man.

The 61-year-old Sprigle headed to Washington, DC, where he boarded a segregated train headed south. He wrote, "I quit being white, and free, and an American citizen when I climbed aboard that Jim Crow coach."

White had arranged for John Wesley Dobbs, a 66-year-old southern civil rights and political leader, to lead Sprigle on a nearly 4,000-mile journey to visit mostly poor Black residents of the Deep South. Sprigle was accepted into their homes—and accepted as a Black man—because he was with Dobbs, whom they knew and respected.

Sprigle presented a devastating picture of life in the South for African Americans. The articles detailing his journey ran on the front page of the *Post-Gazette*. Its editor said the articles attracted more readers than any other. The series was published across the nation and carried in 15 other newspapers including the *Pittsburgh Courier*, America's largest African American—owned news-paper. Sprigle also appeared on the cover of *Time*, which was an honor because it was such a well-known magazine. ■

Anne McClellan, a Women's Air Force service pilot, inside the cockpit of a BT-13; Ann Johnson stands by the plane's wing.

Campaigning for Equality

By June 1948, polls said that Truman could not win the presidential reelection. On June 3, Truman started a two-week train trip from Washington, DC, to Berkeley, California, to accept an honorary degree from the University of California. He would stop at many places along the way so people could meet him and make up their minds about what they'd heard about him. But could he change enough minds? He took the opportunity to attack Congress for blocking everything he'd set out to do to progress civil rights. He needed citizens to come out and vote in November—for him, and against the members of Congress who were stalling progress on rights for all Americans.

The KKK operated openly in the South, conducting well-attended marches and demonstrations.

Terror in the Night

A week after Truman set off, two Alabama Girl Scout training camps with Black and white participants were raided by the KKK.

Late in the evening on June 8, hooded Klan members terrorized Black Girl Scout leaders being trained by two white instructors at Camp Blossom Hill in Birmingham. They woke the women up, demanded everyone's names, and went through their wallets. The men warned the women to leave the premises within 24 hours.

Two nights later, on June 10, the Klan frightened a group of sleeping women at Camp Pauline Bray Fletcher in Bessemer. The circumstances were identical: Black Girl Scout leaders were being trained by two white instructors. The hooded invaders tore through the women's purses and copied down their personal information. The training was stopped the next day and all the shaken women were sent home.

No one would ever be arrested for these attacks, despite investigations by local police and the FBI. Abe Berkowitz, a Birmingham attorney, would form a group of civic and business groups to demand better protection from the Klan. Alabama governor Jim Folsom, Sr., would sign an "anti-masking bill" the following year, attempting to reduce Klan activity.

A Victory for Women

Truman signed the Women's Armed Services **Integration** Act into law on June 12, allowing women to permanently serve in the U.S. military. The bill had struggled in Congress since January. Many congressmen felt that women should only serve in the reserves, or noncombat posts, so they could be observed before being sent into combat.

After much debate, the act allowing women to serve in both the reserves and the regular armed

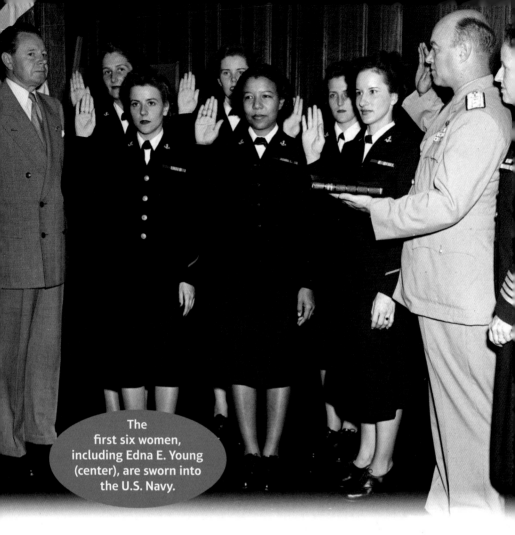

The first six women, including Edna E. Young (center), are sworn into the U.S. Navy.

forces was passed by the Senate on May 26 and by the House of Representatives on June 2.

Previously, women could serve in the military, but primarily in segregated "women only" units. And often their positions were designated for emergency service; once the crisis ended, they were discharged. The Women's Armed Services Integration Act did include some restrictions: Not all positions open to men were available to women, and enlistment and promotional opportunities were limited. However, this represented an opportunity for women to become permanent military members and to receive military benefits. The act included African American women, but they remained segregated. The navy would swear in its first six female members on July 7. Edna Earle Young, an African American woman, was among the inductees.

An armed forces recruitment poster encourages women to sign up.

Miracle Victory

World heavyweight boxing champion Joe Louis managed a miracle victory against challenger Jersey Joe Walcott on June 25, 1948. The champ rose up from a knockout by Walcott in the third round, and he knocked Walcott out in the eleventh round to retain his title. Louis had been behind on all judges' scorecards.

Around 42,000 people flocked to Yankee Stadium to see Louis fight. He weighed 213-and-½ pounds, the heaviest of his career at that time.

Louis had earned the heavyweight title on June 22, 1937. World War II interrupted his career, and he joined the army. Because he was a celebrity, he was placed in the Special Services Division rather than into combat. He traveled more than 22,000 miles, staging 96 boxing exhibitions in front of two million soldiers.

Louis was also used as a promotional tool to recruit African Americans into the racially segregated army. Asked about his decision to serve, Louis said he did experience racism, despite being famous, on more than one occasion. He was awarded the Legion of Merit (a military honor rarely awarded to enlisted soldiers) for his "incalculable contribution to the general morale." Receiving this award gave him immediate release from military service on October 1, 1945.

The years had taken their toll on Louis's skills, but he was too proud to quit. He fought Walcott in 1947 and won, although many people felt he did not deserve it. The June 1948 fight was a rematch.

After the fight, Louis announced his retirement, but he ended up back in the ring years later.

Champion Joe Louis (right) and challenger Joe Walcott tussle in their battle for the world heavyweight title.

Governor Thomas E. Dewey wins the presidential nomination at the Republican National Convention on June 25, 1948.

Republicans Meet

The Republican National Convention met June 21–25 at a convention hall in West Philadelphia. The delegates nominated New York governor Thomas Edmund Dewey as their candidate for president. Governor Earl Warren of California was nominated as vice president. Their plan shared many similarities with Truman's agenda, including a federal anti-lynching law and federal civil rights legislation. The plan also featured federal aid to states for low-cost housing, armed forces integration, labor reform, and ending the poll tax.

In Dewey's acceptance speech he said, "To me, to be a Republican in this hour is to dedicate one's life to the freedom of men."

The question remained: If Republicans believed in the freedom of men, why had the Republicans in Congress blocked Truman's civil rights efforts? The answer had to lie in politics.

Pressure

Frustrated by Truman's lack of action toward desegregating the military despite calling for a new draft, A. Philip Randolph created the League for Non-Violent Civil Disobedience Against Military Segregation on June 26. The group called for an executive order ending military segregation before August 16. If this did not happen, Randolph would begin the campaign encouraging African American youth to refuse to register for the draft.

Nomination

The Democratic National Convention was held in Philadelphia July 12–14. Walter White called all the newspapers denouncing the Southern Democrats. The Democratic Party would not permit racism to dictate its philosophy. The Southern Democrats generated a lot of loud grumbling for the first two days of the convention, and the third day proved to be too much for them.

A Little Higher

Mahalia Jackson's gospel, or church-inspired, song "Move On Up a Little Higher," composed by Reverend William Herbert Brewster, appeared on the Billboard charts in 1948. Recorded and released in 1947, this uplifting song went on to sell eight million copies. This was an astonishing feat for a gospel song!

Reverend Brewster originally wrote the song to depict the Christian's upward journey on the ladder to heaven. But the song's aspirational lyrics and Mahalia Jackson's powerful delivery made for an inspiring post–World War II anthem of Black activism.

Mahalia Jackson's inspiring song helped boost African American spirits and determination.

Southern Democrats' reaction to the civil rights platform at the Democratic National Convention.

On July 14, it was time to decide on the civil rights issue. Northern Democrats pushed for civil rights to be part of the official Democratic plan, while the Southern Democrats resisted. They attempted to introduce their modified plan, only to meet hisses and boos from the crowd. The vote was taken, and the issue of civil rights was officially included in the Democratic plan. Three dozen Southern Democrats walked out of the convention, including Thurmond and Wright. President Truman easily won the nomination as the party's candidate in their absence. Truman received 75 percent of the delegates' votes.

Sow Your Turnips

Truman took the stage to accept his nomination at 1:45 a.m. on July 15, entering to the presidential anthem "Hail to the Chief." It was an exhilarating moment for him, but it was also a defining moment. Congress had stopped meeting for the year weeks ago, leaving most of Truman's agenda untouched. His approval rating was down to 36 percent, largely thanks to his inability to get things done. Truman did something in his speech that had never been done by a presidential nominee before. He called Congress back into session.

He had the power to do this, thanks to Article II, Section 3, of the Constitution.

Truman was challenging the Republicans to live up to the platform they had voted on at their June convention. If they really stood for civil rights, here was the chance to prove it. "They can do this job in 15 days, if they want to do it." he stated. That two-week session would begin on "Turnip Day," taken from an old Missouri saying, "On the twenty-sixth of July, **sow** your turnips, wet or dry." ▪

A jubilant President Truman accepts the Democratic nomination for president on July 15, 1948.

Progressive Party candidate Henry Wallace attracts the support of many youths.

5

Progress and Problems

The Dixiecrats held their convention in Birmingham, Alabama, on July 17 with 6,000 attendees. They nominated J. Strom Thurmond as their candidate for president and Fielding L. Wright as his running mate. The Dixiecrats did not formally declare themselves as a separate political party. They said they were "recommending" that state Democratic parties vote for the Thurmond-Wright ticket.

Progressive Keynote Address

On July 23–35, a third political party, which had been started by a new organization called the Progressive Citizens of America, held their convention.

Some leading Black activists attended this convention because they felt they had lost their voices in America.

Shirley Graham, an author, playwright, composer, and activist, gave the first keynote address by an African American at a political convention. She discussed the history of Black Americans and said she had come to the convention as an American claiming the rights of citizenship for Black Americans. She said that Henry Wallace, the Progressive candidate, was "the only candidate who advocated demolishing Jim Crow, and the only candidate who wanted to invest in the Black community and not war against people of color abroad."

She proposed a plan that was adopted at the convention. It demanded an end to Jim Crow, "full equality" for Black Americans, an end to the segregated military, anti-lynching legislation, anti—poll tax legislation, and funding for healthcare and housing.

Alice Coachman

Alice Coachman became the first Black woman to win an Olympic gold medal at the 1948 Summer Olympics in London, United Kingdom. The 25-year-old track and field star had spent years of her peak athletic ability unable to compete due to World War II—both the 1940 and the 1944 Games had been canceled. Finally, she was able to show the world her talent, leaping to a record-breaking height of 5 feet, 6-and-⅛ inches in the high jump.

At the Olympics, King George VI, father of Queen Elizabeth II, awarded Coachman her medal. When she returned to the United States, she met President Harry S. Truman and former first lady Eleanor Roosevelt. Coachman retired from sports, but that didn't stop the Coca-Cola Company from asking her to be a spokesperson in 1952. She became the first African American to receive an endorsement deal.

Coachman wanted to support young athletes and older, retired Olympic veterans. She started the Alice Coachman Track and Field Foundation to do so. She was honored as one of the 100 greatest Olympians in history at the 1996 Summer Olympic Games in Atlanta, Georgia.

Alice Coachman (center) waits to receive her gold medal at the Summer Olympics on August 7, 1948.

Other African American leaders who attended the conference and worked tirelessly supporting the party included Charlotta Bass. In 1952, Bass would agree to be the vice presidential candidate on the Progressive ticket, becoming the first Black woman on a major party ticket.

Turnip Day

July 26 was Turnip Day—and Truman chose this day to use his executive power as much as he could, despite the problematic Congress.

Truman issued two executive orders. The first, Executive Order 9980, was called "Regulations Governing Fair Employment Practices Within the Federal Establishment." This order desegregated the federal workforce.

The second, Executive Order 9981, was called "Establishing the President's Committee on Equality of Treatment and Opportunity in the Armed Forces." The order declared that "there shall be equality of treatment and opportunity for all persons in the armed forces without regard to race, color, religion, or national origin." A committee would investigate the ways to best achieve this.

However, the wording was vague. Did the president's desire for the equality of treatment and opportunity in the armed forces mean that he envisioned

Truman challenges Congressional members on Turnip Day to pass legislation on civil rights.

the end of segregation? When he was asked this three days later, Truman answered, "Yes."

Congress started their session on Turnip Day. Republican members were in a bind. How could they not act on what they had pledged to do at their convention? If Republicans failed to pass anything, Truman would call them deceitful. This would certainly hurt their chances of winning the election. But if they did pass civil rights legislation, Truman would take the credit and use it to fuel his election campaign.

Truman on the campaign trail for reelection. He was determined to travel as much as possible.

The congressional Republicans argued about what to do. Some felt that they should act on a few measures to please certain voters. But others were against this.

After 11 days, Congress sent two bills to Truman for signing. One bill was to curb the rising costs of living, and the other was to encourage new housing construction. Truman signed both bills but called them "inadequate."

Truman's Turnip Day challenge had energized Truman's Democratic supporters, and the Republican Party was on the defensive. Even the Republicans' own presidential candidate, Thomas E. Dewey, praised Truman's special session of Congress.

Would this be enough for Truman to come from behind and win?

Slim Chance

Because of the split within the Democratic Party, many polls gave Truman a slim chance of winning. There was tremendous struggling and legal battling by Democrats and Dixiecrats over who would be listed as the presidential nominee on the southern ballots. The result was that both Truman and Thurmond would be listed, except for the state of Alabama, where Truman was left off.

Perez v. Sharp

Perez v. Sharp was a 1948 California lawsuit filed by an interracial couple who wished to get married. California had a law dating back to 1850 enforcing segregation by banning marriage between interracial couples.

Andrea Perez (a Mexican American woman) and Sylvester Davis (an African American man) were a Los Angeles couple who filed for a marriage license with the county clerk of Los Angeles. On the application, Andrea Perez listed her race as "white," and Sylvester Davis marked down "Negro." People of Mexican ancestry were classified white because of their Spanish heritage.

W. G. Sharp, the county clerk, refused to issue their license. Perez petitioned the California Supreme Court to compel the issuance of the license. Perez and Davis were Catholics, and the Catholic church was fine with marrying them. How could the state forbid their religious marriage?

On October 1, 1948, by a narrow margin of 4–3, the court agreed that they had no right to restrict a marriage due to prejudice. Marriage was a fundamental right provided by the U.S. Constitution and could not be withheld.

Seal of the California Supreme Court.

But the Democratic Party had another problem: It had no money. Truman pledged to go on a campaign trip after Labor Day, heading all over the country to raise both votes and donations. He loved traveling, especially on trains. Truman also loved getting out there and meeting the people face-to-face. He wrote to his sister, "It will be the greatest campaign any President ever made. Win, lose, or draw people will know where I stand."

Days before the election, Truman addresses citizens of Harlem, New York City, as he accepts the Franklin D. Roosevelt Award.

We must look forward to great tomorrows

6

Triumph

During Truman's reelection campaign journey, he avoided speaking about the civil rights issue. One of his speechwriters had advised him that the issue "had already done enough damage to the party." Thurmond tried coaxing the president into a debate on civil rights to be held somewhere in the South, but Truman ignored him.

However, Truman's actions spoke for him. In Waco, Texas, he shook hands with a Black woman who was a well-known member of a nearby interracial group. There were some boos in the crowd, but cheers drowned them out. In Dallas, Texas, segregation was eliminated from his speech to 20,000 cheering racially mixed people. Truman also met with Black supporters informally.

Truman had the company of a young Texas congressman named Lyndon B. Johnson on his train ride through Texas. An endorsement from a Texas politician gave Truman a boost, and an endorsement from the president gave Johnson's campaign for Senate a boost. "Send Lyndon Johnson to the Senate," Truman declared to a Texas crowd.

Dewey, who was also campaigning, also did not speak about civil rights. He had a good civil rights record in New York, which the Republican National Committee advertised in Black newspapers, but he avoided the topic in his speeches. Dewey's campaign did not consider that civil rights were far more welcome in New York than in the South.

Dewey and his family were sure he was going to win. His mother, Annie, wrote to him, asking where she and his father could stay for Dewey's inauguration. He answered that he was not sure if there was enough room at the White House. While some African American newspapers throughout the country endorsed Truman, many endorsed Dewey instead, embracing his civil rights record and criticizing Truman's inability to get things done.

Newsweek magazine published a poll of 50 leading political reporters throughout the country. All of them said that Dewey would win. But Truman never stopped believing in himself, and he campaigned harder.

Dixiecrats at the States' Rights Convention boo a Henry Wallace supporter protesting outside.

No Chance

Thurmond had no chance at winning and little chance of earning enough votes to have any effect on the election results. Some southern politicians stayed with the Democratic Party because of this, even though they agreed with the Dixiecrat platform.

Wallace, who also had no chance, campaigned regardless. He made reaching out to Black voters a priority, especially in the South. White southerners did not like this, and they threw rotten eggs at Wallace at his appearances. Wallace's trip brought the ugliness of segregation to the forefront of people's minds. Police had to keep Wallace's Black supporters safe from the white protesters, and there were several violent outbreaks.

President Truman's campaign trail heads across Harlem's 125th Street on October 29, 1948, to cheers.

A Religious Occasion

On October 29, four days before the election, Truman broke his silence on the issue of civil rights. He was in Harlem, a neighborhood in New York City, outdoors in Dorrance Brooks Square, at a meeting of the Council of Negro Clergymen. They were awarding Truman with the Franklin D. Roosevelt Memorial Award for his civil rights record. There was a crowd of more than 60,000 people.

When Truman rose to speak, students on the edge of the crowd from nearby City College yelled out in support, but the cheers were met with silence.

Sun Bowl Discrimination

On November 19, 1948, the Lafayette College football team, the Lafayette Leopards, in Easton, Pennsylvania, was invited to play in the 1949 Sun Bowl, to be held in El Paso, Texas, at the Texas College of Mines (now the University of Texas at El Paso). But when the Sun Bowl Committee realized that the Leopards included a Black player named David Showell, the invitation changed, now with the condition that Showell not play. (After high school, Showell joined the U.S. Army and was a member of the Tuskegee Airmen during World War II before attending Lafayette College.)

On November 23, the faculty voted to decline the invitation because of Showell's exclusion. Lafayette students were upset. Nearly 1,000 students began a demonstration on the campus and headed to Centre Square in downtown Easton in protest of the discrimination toward Showell. Several students sent a telegram to President Truman that read: "Denied Sun Bowl game because we have a Negro on our team. Is that democracy?" signed by the Lafayette College students. Despite the student protests, Lafayette did not end up playing in the Sun Bowl.

Lafayette College's 1948 football team.

No one in the crowd joined in, and the students stopped shouting. This seemed like bad news to Truman and his staff. But when they looked at the crowd, they saw the positive reason for the silence. The crowd was praying—some with their heads down, some kneeling. Philleo Nash, who had helped create the President's Committee on Civil Rights, and who had arrived in New York at five that morning to go over Truman's speech, said, "They were praying for the president, and they were praying for their own civil rights. And they thought it was a religious occasion."

Truman spoke to the group solemnly, recommitting himself to the civil rights cause. It was the first anniversary of the submission of the Committee on Civil Rights report. He spoke about the committee's proposals and how he'd submitted them to Congress. Truman closed by saying he intended to keep moving toward the goal of equal rights "with every ounce of strength and determination I have."

End Results

The last poll before the election showed Truman losing to Dewey. Not one poll had shown him winning. Nevertheless, Truman seemed in good spirits when he headed home to Independence, Missouri, to hear the election night results. He heard the early returns and fell asleep. A Secret Service agent woke him up at midnight to tell him he was winning in Massachusetts. Truman told him to stop worrying, go to bed, and they would get up early in the morning.

Truman woke up again at 4 a.m. on November 3 and learned he was winning the popular vote by two million. Truman was headed back to the White House for four more years, despite all the polls that had said otherwise. One newspaper, the *Chicago Tribune*, even got the outcome wrong, printing before the results were final because of the grim predictions. Truman's train stopped in St. Louis on the way back to Washington, and he was handed a copy of the newspaper with the headline DEWEY DEFEATS TRUMAN. He smiled and held it up high, posing for a picture.

Negro National League

The Negro National League (NNL) ended on November 30, 1948, at the end of its season. Major League Baseball had desegregated the year prior, and Black players displaying great talent were being recruited by MLB. This was wonderful for African American civil rights and equality, but it spelled the decline of Negro Major Leagues, which had operated successfully since 1920. When the NNL dissolved, three of its six teams folded. The other three teams joined the Negro American League, which ended after its 1962 season.

The 1948 Negro League East All-Stars pose just before the 1948 East-West Game.

A victorious Truman playfully holds a premature headline from the *Chicago Daily Tribune*, wrongly declaring his defeat by Dewey.

Truman won reelection with 303 electoral votes to Dewey's 189. The popular vote came out 24,105,695 for Truman; 21,969,170 for Dewey; 1,169,021 for Thurmond; and 1,156,103 for Wallace.

Everyone said that Truman alone was responsible for his come-from-behind victory—and for a large part, he was. But he was proud and heartened that he carried the Black vote, receiving more than 75 percent of their ballots. African American voters supported Truman in the election just as he supported them in the federal government. And he would continue to do so.

ME PRESIDENT TRUMAN
PION OF HUMAN RIGHTS

Truman is welcomed at a ceremony in the Virgin Islands.

The Legacy of 1948 in Civil Rights History

The civil rights movement was just taking shape in 1948, and President Harry S. Truman helped set its course. His support for Black citizens hadn't been seen before in the federal government, and he not only made progress, but also gave African Americans a boost in their faith that the government cared about them. Truman's work against discrimination and segregation influenced civil rights and future presidents for decades to come. His rejection of the "separate but equal" policy in relation to the armed forces opened the door for ending the doctrine completely.

When President Lyndon B. Johnson—who Truman had ridden with on a train through Texas 16 years earlier—signed the 1964 Civil Rights Act into law, one of Johnson's aides commented, "Truman's hand steadied his."

Between 1948 and 1964, the civil rights movement progressed and flourished due to the devotion of civil rights groups and African American citizens determined to challenge discrimination in the courts and through nonviolent protests. Thurgood Marshall worked tirelessly to wage a legal war against segregation, and in 1954 he secured his most famous victory in *Brown v. Board of Education*, which ended public school segregation. Marshall was also instrumental in striking down segregation in public transportation and restaurants.

By 1960, another group rose to prominence in the civil rights movement: students. Their nonviolent protests proved crucial in desegregating lunch

President Lyndon B. Johnson signs the Civil Rights Act on July 2, 1964.

Members of the Student Nonviolent Coordinating Committee at a 1966 news conference.

counters across the South. Uniting in groups such as the Student Nonviolent Coordinating Committee (SNCC), these students would play major roles in ending discrimination and earning equal rights for all citizens.

At the end of 1948, Black Americans still faced a long and uphill battle for civil rights, but the progress that was made at the federal level helped set the stage for more progress in the coming years. ■

Shirley Chisholm

An American politician, educator, and author, Shirley Chisholm was the first Black woman elected to the United States Congress. She became the first Black candidate to seek a major party's nomination for president of the United States and the first woman to run for the Democratic Party's nomination.

Shirley Anita St. Hill was born in New York City on November 30, 1924. Her parents were **immigrants** from British Guiana and Barbados. Both parents had to work to support their family. Shirley and her two younger sisters were sent on a ship to Barbados to

U.S. Representative Shirley Chisholm of Brooklyn declares her entry for the Democratic nomination for the presidency on January 25, 1972.

live with their grandmother when Shirley was five.

Attending a one-room schoolhouse in Barbados, Shirley received an excellent education. She and her sisters returned to New York on May 19, 1934.

Shirley was exposed to politics early on. Her father was dedicated to the rights of **union** members. Before that, in Barbados, she had witnessed her community supporting Barbados workers' rights.

Shirley attended the well-regarded, integrated Girls' High School in Brooklyn. Shirley then attended Brooklyn College, where she won awards for

New York congresswoman Shirley Chisholm in 1970.

supporting the integration of Black soldiers during World War II. She also campaigned for courses focusing on African American history, and for more women to be involved in the student government.

Shirley married Conrad O. Chisholm, a Jamaican immigrant, in 1949. He became a private investigator. Shirley earned her master's degree in elementary education in 1952 from Teachers College of Columbia University.

debating. She was a member of the Harriet Tubman Society.

In the Harriet Tubman Society, Shirley worked for inclusion, especially

Shirley Chisholm State Park in Brooklyn, NY.

"I am not the candidate of Black America, although I am Black and proud. I am not the candidate of the women's movement of this country, although I am a woman and equally proud of that. I am the candidate of the people and my presence before you symbolizes a new era in American political history." —SHIRLEY CHISHOLM

Becoming known as an expert on issues involving early education and child **welfare**, Chisholm worked in education from 1953 to 1959. In 1964, Chisholm ran for a seat in the New York State Assembly. She served in the Assembly from 1965 to 1968.

Congresswoman Shirley Chisolm in her Brooklyn office, 1974.

Chisholm was elected as the Democratic National Committeewoman from New York State in 1968. That same year, she ran for the U.S. House of Representatives from New York's 12th congressional district and became the first Black woman elected to Congress.

A well-respected and hard-working congresswoman, Chisholm declared her candidacy for president on January 25, 1972. Unfortunately, her campaign was underfunded, and many voters did not regard her as a serious contender. Nevertheless, she won the respect of the nation.

Chisholm and C. Delores Tucker cofounded the National Congress of Black Women (NCBW) in 1984 and served as its founding chairs. Dedicated to enriching the lives and development of African American women and their families, the NCBW continues to thrive to this day.

In 1993, Chisholm was inducted into the National Women's Hall of Fame.

She passed away on January 1, 2005. A Forever stamp was issued in her honor on January 31, 2014. Barack Obama awarded Chisholm the Presidential Medal of Freedom on November 24, 2015.

TIMELINE

The Year in Civil Rights

1948

JANUARY 7

President Truman speaks up for civil rights during his 1948 State of the Union address, putting him at odds with much of Congress.

FEBRUARY 7

Southern governors gather in Wakulla Springs, Florida, to discuss strategy against civil rights. Governor Wright of Mississippi proposes that they immediately leave the Democratic Party and start their own.

MARCH 2

Hooded members of the Ku Klux Klan burn a cross on the courthouse lawn in Wrightsville, Georgia, to frighten Black citizens from voting.

MARCH 13

Southern governors met in Washington, DC. They unanimously pass a resolution denouncing the Democratic Party leadership for its support of civil rights.

APRIL 20

Roy Campanella becomes the first African American catcher in Major League Baseball.

MAY 3

The Supreme Court hands down a landmark decision against housing discrimination in *Shelley v. Kraemer*.

JUNE 12

Truman signs the Women's Armed Services Integration Act into law, allowing women to permanently serve in the U.S. military.

JULY 26

Truman chose Turnip Day to issue two executive orders to desegregate the federal workforce and equality in the armed forces.

AUGUST 7

Alice Coachman becomes the first Black woman to win an Olympic gold medal at the Summer Olympics in London, United Kingdom.

OCTOBER 1

The Supreme Court rules in the *Perez v. Sharp* case that they had no right to restrict a marriage due to racial prejudice.

NOVEMBER 2

Truman wins reelection, receiving more than 75 percent of the African American vote.

NOVEMBER 30

The Negro National League dissolves after their season ends, following the desegregation of Major League Baseball.

GLOSSARY

activist (AK-tuh-vist) a person who works to bring about political or social change

amendment (uh-MEND-muhnt) a change that is made to a law or legal document

citizenship (SIT-i-zuhn-ship) the legal status of being a citizen of a country, with full rights to live, work, and vote there

civil rights (SIV-uhl rites) the individual rights that all members of a democratic society have to freedom and equal treatment under the law

commission (kuh-MISH-uhn) a group of people who meet to solve a particular problem or do certain tasks

Confederate (kuhn-FED-ur-it) of or having to do with the Confederacy, or the group of 11 states that declared independence from the rest of the U.S. just before the Civil War

delegate (DEL-i-git) someone who represents other people at a meeting or in a legislature

democracy (di-MAH-kruh-see) a form of government in which the people choose their leaders in elections

desegregation (dee-seg-ruh-GAY-shuhn) doing away with the practice of separating people of different races in schools, restaurants, and other public places

discrimination (dis-krim-uh-NAY-shuhn) prejudice or unfair behavior to others based on differences such as in race, gender, or age

draft (draft) to make someone join the armed forces

endorsement (en-DORS-ment) to support or approve of someone or something

executive order (egg-ZEK-yuh-tiv awr-der) an order having the force of law issued by the president of the United States

federal (FED-ur-uhl) national government, as opposed to state or local government

immigrant (IM-i-gruhnt) someone who moves from one country to another and settles there

integration (in-ti-GRAY-shuhn) the act or practice of making facilities or an organization open to people of all races and ethnic groups

interracial (in-tur-RAY-shuhl) involving people of different races

Jim Crow (jim kro) the practice of segregating Black people in the United States, named after a character who degraded African American life and culture

Ku Klux Klan (KOO kluks KLAN) a secret organization in the United States that uses threats and violence to achieve its goal of white supremacy; also called the Klan or the KKK

labor (LAY-bur) workers as a group, especially those who do physical work

lynching (LIN-ching) a sometimes public murder by a group of people, often involving hanging

petition (puh-TISH-uhn) a letter signed by many people asking those in power to change their policy or actions or explaining how the signers feel about a certain issue or situation

plantation (plan-TAY-shuhn) a large farm found in warm climates where crops such as coffee, rubber, and cotton are grown

prejudice (PREJ-uh-dis) immovable, unreasonable, or unfair opinion about someone based on the person's race, religion, or other characteristic

primary (PRYE-mair-ee) an election to choose a party candidate who will run in the general election

resolution (rez-uh-LOO-shuhn) a formal expression of opinion, will, or intent voted by an official body or assembled group

segregation (seg-ruh-GAY-shuhn) the act or practice of keeping people or groups apart

sow (soh) to scatter seeds over the ground so they will grow; to plant

unanimous (yoo-NAN-uh-muhs) agreed on by everyone

unconstitutional (un-kahn-stuh-TOO-shuhn-uhl) not in keeping with the basic principles or laws set forth in the U.S. Constitution

union (YOON-yuhn) an organized group of workers set up to help improve such things as working conditions, wages, and health benefits

welfare (WEL-fair) money or help given by a government to people who are in need

white supremacist (wite su-PREM-uh-sist) a person with the belief that the white race is better than other races and that white people should have control over people of other races

BIBLIOGRAPHY

Berman, William. *The Politics of Civil Rights in the Truman Administration*. Ohio: Ohio State University Press, 1970.

Davis, Michelle H. *Dixiegops: The Untold Story of the Dixiecrat-Republican Coalition*. Texas: Living Blue Texas, 2021.

"Democratic National Convention," *Newsweek*, XXXII, Number 4 (July 26, 1948), 17–24.

Gardner, Michael R. *Harry Truman and Civil Rights: Moral Courage and Political Risks*. Carbondale and Edwardsville: Southern Illinois University Press, 2002.

Hurns, Walter McCloskey. "The Response of the Black Community in Mississippi to the Dixiecrat Movement of 1948." Morehead, Kentucky: Morehead State University, 1972.

Kirkendall, Richard S., ed. *The Truman Period as a Research Field*. Columbia, Missouri: *University of Missouri Press*, 1967.

McCoy, Donald R. and Richard T. Ruetten. *Quest and Response: Minority Rights and the Truman Administration*. Kansas: University Press of Kansas, 1973.

McCullough, David. *Truman*. New York: Simon & Schuster, 1992.

Moon, Henry Lee. *Balance of Power: The Negro Vote*. New York: Doubleday and Company, 1969.

Popham, John H. "Negro in South Still Lags in Power," *The New York Times*, February 15, 1948.

Popham, John H. "Gov. Wright Bids Negroes Be Quiet," *The New York Times*, May 10, 1948.

Popham, John H. "Southerners Name Thurman to Lead Anti-Truman Fight." *The New York Times*, July 18, 1948.

Shogan, Robert. *Harry Truman and the Struggle for Racial Justice*. Kansas: University Press of Kansas, 2013.

Truman, Harry S. *Memoirs: Years of Trial and Hope*, Vol. 2. New York: Doubleday and Company, 1956.

Sipuel v. Board of Regents of Univ. of Okla., Library of Congress, tile.loc.gov

Sprigle, Ray. "I Was a Negro in the South for 30 Days," old.post-gazette.com/sprigle/

Thurmond, J. Strom, chairman. "Southern Governors' Conference Committee Report on Civil Rights," tigerprints.clemson.edu

Truman, Harry S. Executive Order 9918, usa.usembassy.de/etexts/democrac/35.htm

Truman, Harry S. "Special Message to Universal Declaration of Human Rights." United Nations Library & Archives, Geneva, libraryresources.unog.ch/udhr

"To Secure These Rights: The Report of the President's Committee on Civil Rights," trumanlibrary.gov/library/to-secure-these-rights

Women are sworn in as permanent members of the U.S. Army.

INDEX

About the Author

Selene Castrovilla is an acclaimed, award-winning author. Her five books on the American Revolution for young readers include Scholastic's *The Founding Mothers*. Selene has been a meticulous researcher of American history since 2003. She has expanded her exploration into the civil rights movement, as well as the Civil War, in a forthcoming book. A frequent speaker about our nation's evolution, she is equally comfortable with audiences of children and adults. Please visit selenecastrovilla.com.

PHOTO CREDITS